The Scent of Man

ARROWSMITH

PRESS

The Scent of Man

ISBN: 979-8-9915254-5-9

Library of Congress Control Number: 2025914183

Boston — New York — San Francisco — Baghdad
San Juan — Kyiv — Istanbul — Santiago, Chile
Beijing — Paris — London — Cairo — Madrid
Milan — Melbourne — Jerusalem — Darfur

11 Chestnut St.
Medford, MA 02155
arrowsmithpress@gmail.com
www.arrowsmithpress.com

The sixty-ninth Arrowsmith book was typeset & designed by
Bella Bennett for Askold Melnyczuk & Alex Johnson in Plantin

Cover photograph by Tadeusz Dąbrowski

The Scent of Man

Tadeusz Dąbrowski

Translated from the Polish by Antonia Lloyd-Jones

Contents

Sentence

It's as if you'd woken in a locked cell and found
in your pocket a slip of paper, and on it a single sentence
in a language you don't know.

And you'd be sure this sentence was the key to your
life. Also to this cell.

And you'd spend years trying to decipher the sentence,
until finally you'd understand it. But after a while
you'd realize you got it wrong, and the sentence meant
something else entirely. And so you'd have two sentences.

Then three, and four, and ten, until you'd created a new language.

And in that language you'd write the novel of your life.
And once you'd reached old age, you'd notice the door of the cell
was open. You'd go out into the world. You'd walk the length and
    breadth of it,

until in the shade of a massive tree you'd yearn
for that one single sentence in a language you don't know.

Passion

For Wacław Tkaczuk

My friend came to the meeting early.
Instead of taking me for a whisky in his customary way,
he proposed an exhibition of Renaissance masters.
He viewed the paintings in focused haste, to avoid
too much looking, so something unclear would still remain
of this brilliance for a lonely evening. My old friend,
with whom I've chattered and been silent on the topic
of poetry for hundreds of hours, took me to an exhibition where
I saw *Portrait of an Unknown Poet*, and in the next room
The Passion by an unknown artist from Lombardy.
My friend, sick with cancer, took me to an exhibition
of late Renaissance masters.

Mondrian

White comes up to black: do not deceive
yourself. Green says to red: we're doing the same thing,
but differently. Yellow meets yellow: take a look
inside yourself. Blue is silent: I am neither
twilight nor the ocean deep, I am here to make
sure green doesn't change into hope or grass.

★ ★ ★

My masculine face
is halfway feminine.

As I get older
in the barber's mirror,
those two faces of mine––
she and he––are languid,

they pass each other indifferently
in the hallways of glances.
They engender wrinkles.

They might resemble
a grumpy old married couple.

But maybe they do in fact
love each other, seeing
one is constantly
saying to the other:

I've got to die before you.

Hall of Mirrors

It's very dangerous to know
too many words.

Each of them has its
flip side, which
also has its flip side
and so on ad infinitum.

A mirrored hall of words.

The sad side of happiness
and the sad side of sorrow.

Words with ears
on the inside.

A world thickly coated
in panels of words
is frightening.

You don't know what's happening
behind the wall or under the floor.

Crayons

A boy and a girl in a train compartment. She
is absorbed by a coloring book, he by her, he's watching
and handing her crayons. Beside them sits a man
who betrayed his wife today. Throughout
the journey he sleeps. He's sleeping off a hangover. At last

he gets up and leaves the compartment. By accident
he spills the crayons.

Heel

It's not that I didn't like the taste of our bread,
it's just that the slicer cut it into thick chunks
because some old bread was lying in it, a heel that made
the machine treat our loaf like a continuation
of that loaf, to sum up: I was given––
instead of a loaf cut into thin
slices––several pieces, which I meekly took
home, because you don't waste bread, but
they couldn't be divided into thinner pieces, they crumbled
in our hands like the tree of life in a lumber mill,
so it wasn't my fault or yours,
or even the fault of that alien heel which finally
turned our bread into sawdust.

Such Love

Such a silence that everything can be heard,
such a brilliance that nothing can be seen,
such warmth that shivers abound,
such sweetness that bitterness reigns.

Such peace that everything vexes,
such language that other words are jabber.

Such a love that nothing can be felt.

Jam Jars

*In classical physics, the past is assumed to exist as
a definite series of events, but according to quantum
physics (...) only as a spectrum of possibilities.*

—Stephen Hawking

Too often they kept on surfacing suddenly, stifling
like a blazing summer in childhood, scalding like the first
stranger's touch, enticing like all those whoreson
numbers in an old address book, like music and singing
audible at twilight from a distant part of town.
In they pressed through every single skin pore, so
I shut them up in separate jam jars and took them down
to the cellar. Sometimes I remove a drop from each one,
mix them in a glass of water and look to see what would happen,
if. But ever more often, in the total silence,
I can hear something roaring and hissing in the cellar. One day
the jars will break, and the memories will merge into a single
oily puddle, which I shall enter, as into fire.

★ ★ ★

I thought love died more impressively
of a heart attack or AIDS, but it goes away

casually like a person
who's lost, but is still

unaware of it.

This is the End

Ever since you left, I've felt like an old
Jim Morrison. I sit here on the can, humming
the hits I'll never record.

I thought by now I'd swept out every last
reminder of you, but now in the corner I can see
your tampon. I'm pretending I don't know anything about it. It's

pretending it can't see me either. This is
the end. Meanwhile outside the window
there's red snow.

Through and Through

How many times in marriage did I kneel before my old
record collection and not know what to choose.

With each successive woman since, I've also knelt
and not known what to choose, because I knew all the records
by heart.

I've just transferred them to a new life.
They're standing in pedantic array. She asks
what I'd like to play her, and I kneel before the shelf

surprised that of all the records, which I know through and through,
I don't know what to choose.

Boots

"I must take them to the cobbler,
they've only got slightly
worn-down heels,"

says my mother, holding
my winter boots
from the days when I had a wife.

Dirtbag

The border between
a decent person and a dirtbag
is thin as a hair,

as the scratch that each day
I mark with a fingernail
on my brow, vertical and

horizontal. My dirtbag
cleanses the backstreets of thoughts
in which the decent person
would never set

foot. My dirtbag
allows the decent
person to retain

purity.

Homefulness

The same nine paces from living room to kitchen
and four from kitchen to bedroom, covered
daily, by heart, on impulse, with an impetus
paid for at times by brushing a hip against a handle
that was actually a few centimeters
closer (is that habit from a former life?).

Now he covers a zigzag path between
the night store and the tram shelter. They say:
"homeless, drunk, crazy," but he's just walking
from kitchen to living room.

* * *

Talking to a star
you're talking to yourself.

Talking to the wind
you're talking to yourself.

Talking to a stone
you're talking to yourself.

Talking to yourself
you're talking to yourself.

Hilltop

Returning to the very same place,
let it be a hilltop
with a view of the night city

where once you used to be,
when your "whole life"
still lay ahead of you,
when everything was before.

Returning—when it's already after:
irrevocably, decisively.
What a strange feeling it is.

As if you had the gift of prophecy
in a world without time.

Zurich 2016–2019

In Between

I've got a thing about watches,
I've just been watching a film about
the world's most punctual
mechanical clock,
which only gains a
single second a century.

And I'm wondering
how dreadful the world would be
without the stolen minutes;
there'd be no time for
hesitating between im-
and perfective tenses,
affairs after hours,
innocent slippage,
accurate morality,
the balanced truth,
winning by a hair,
or perfect murders.

There'd even be no gaps
in time for writing a poem
in the style of Wisława
Szymborska. What's more:

there'd be no time to
ask you who you are
when you're not there.

Almost There

For several hours it has been desperately beating
against the pane, though the window is ajar. Beyond it
lies its garden. "I'm almost there now,
but something's keeping me tethered, as if I were unstuck

from reality," thinks the fly, choking, and with every
second weakens. It has a terrible death, quite like a man
under ice, who to the bitter end, to the very last
bubble of air in his lungs, feels as if he's

almost there now, but this "almost" makes
a difference. I look at my life to date,
then at my future life, and I am "almost there,"
sitting in an empty room, between two windows

facing onto the garden.

Bouquet

Paulina, the gardener's daughter, cares
about flowers doomed to die.

If I bring her a bouquet, she frees it
from the ribbons and gently places it in the hospice

of a vase. When the flowers weaken, she trims their stems
and plucks off their wilting leaves. She takes

the dead ones to the compost, from the rest
she forms a new bouquet. Thus disappear in turn:

poppies, anemones, carnations, damnations and
forget-me-nots, until finally all that's left are

gypsophila and Judas' pennies. Paulina,
the gardener's daughter, sees a bouquet in the vase

even when it's not there anymore.

Letter

Yesterday I sent you a letter. And today on the phone
you tell me you are pregnant. I pack up and return,
you greet me at the airport, you're even lovelier than
in my letter that's on its way to you. We build
a house, our child grows, our parents shrink,
then a few years of sweat and tears, in which we prudently
pickle cabbage and gherkins for the ever colder days.
In the coloring book of our life there are fewer and fewer
blank spaces, the crayons grow shorter, we try to be precise,
but even so we go over the lines. We busy ourselves
with everyday matters, and our paths are ever
deeper, they start to look like tunnels. Meanwhile
my letter's on its way to you. You'll open it when
it suits you best.

Grammar

There were no streets on the people,
a heavy sky shrouded the clouds,
the churches rang in empty bells,
sweating sleep tossed and turned in me,
syntax didn't care about the young poets,
there was too much empty fridge in the bottles,
evil women dragged good men into bed.

And then you came, and laid yourself on my
lips like an indicative sentence. Since then words
listen to us intently, hands offer us to each other, and at night
blind stars fix their gaze on us, but now I know
that's normal.

Ars Poetica

They ask me what is poetry,
or what does a poet feel while writing a poem.

My daughter is six months old and her mother's
breast is the whole world to her, physics

and metaphysics. Sometimes we deceive
her with a pacifier, but lately she pulls it out

of her mouth and watches. She's surprised
and focused then, like me as I look at the world

that I've managed
to take out of my mouth.

Break

The arm I shattered on a bike,
meticulously reassembled by surgeons,
is now healing up in pain, and so it will be
for long weeks to come. Over the eastern border
of my country there's a war on, the able skeletons
of men are grabbing weapons and going to get death
or life, in their skulls *yin* and *yang* merge
into one, as if they were parts of a spinning
bullet before it hits the target. Meanwhile my arm
broken in three places is slowly starting to
heal, which means I'll miss out this summer
on bathing in the lake, Sunday trips to the beach,
catching fish, and even the sweet burden of my one-
year-old daughter, who looks at the plaster and twists
her lips into a horseshoe. Meanwhile on the front lines
healthy skeletons are fighting in a righteous cause,
crushing skeletons fighting in an evil cause,
and I know that for three more months I won't be
able to wash myself properly. When I've healed up, I'll be
part of the world's skeleton again, but this
time, if I get shattered, then only for a worthy
aim, my mended arm will grab a weapon and set off
shoulder to shoulder with the freedom fighters, my index
finger will learn to pull the trigger of my rifle
tenderly—such thoughts went shooting through my head
as I lay in the recovery room.

But a few months on, when my plaster was removed,
with trembling hand I showed my little daughter
a plump sparrow perched on too thin a branch.

Żuławy

Do you like Żuławy? I asked her and instantly
heard my own self, but she, amazingly,
threw herself on me and did it so effectively
that we have three adult children now. Of course,

I'm making all this up to feed poetry,
as I speed by car across Żuławy with the future mother of my
three children, when the temptation suddenly seizes me
to interlace the thread of text with the warp of life, so I ask

spontaneously: Do you like Żuławy? But I don't get
any answer.

Love Letter

She cannot, or simply will not go to sleep,
if the raindrops of her fingers are falling on my brow
like the vanguard of a storm that will however pass
to one side. If the warm current of her breath is flowing
into the lagoon of my ear. If even her big
toe is stretching out in my direction
like the nose of a mole. My tiny little woman,
in some sixteen years from now another man
will be lying next to you. I don't know if at the time
I'll still be alive, so I'm shedding this tear now.

Towels

Paulina is going nuts
about how to launder the towels
to make them perfectly white.

Find out how they do it
at hotels, they're able
to launder almost anything,

I advise her, though I'd rather have
a towel that's gone yellow, knowing
the source of the yellow,

than a snow-white one, not knowing
the source of the white.

A Lesser Evil

But it was also
once greater compared
with another lesser

evil. Today I chose
the lesser evil.

I keep it in a jar.

It's got milk teeth already.

Snake

For Zbigniew Herbert

I read everything, because I'm able
to tell facts from fakes.

There are texts one has only to
flip over to the other side
and they become honest.

But mostly reading
demands strenuous labor,
and then I sit with pencil
in hand and draw a boundary
line between paragraphs,
across sentences.

The line is usually long
and narrow, resembling
the snake from a cult game
in archaic cell phones.

Quite often, wanting to separate
truth from falsehood, I have to
cut through the middle of a word.

It takes a steady hand
and precision tools,
let's call them the lancet
of the intellect and the pliers

of conscience. Sometimes
when separated from falsehood
the truth bleeds for a while,
and then dies.

Secret Reading Matter

I take the books left for free recycling mainly for their smell,
I stick my nose among the pages, into business not my own,
then stroll around someone else's home,
peeping into their kitchen and their bedroom. But once
their smell has faded and the book's imbued with mine,
I leave it at a bus stop or in a letter box.
Busy non-stop with their crimes, their love lives,
good and evil, keeping an eye on the time
and the setting, the characters haven't a clue how many books
they're carrying away in their clothing.

Phone Call

My grandma's dying in the hospital on the other side
of the street, and my one-year-old daughter will not go to sleep.

The oldest woman in the family is speaking to me through
the youngest. Only I know Grandma won't peg out until

Basia (who's inherited her bags under the eyes,
now resembling two half-moons) has settled down.

I wait until dawn, but my daughter refuses to give in,
dozily righting herself like Mr. Wobblyman. Finally

I pick her up, give her a firm cuddle and whisper
into the small receiver of her ear: "Sleep now, stop being afraid."

Coffee Without

First coffee without Grandma.
Her body is not yet cold.
It's lukewarm, like this coffee.

First morning without Grandma.
Outside it's raining.
Even if it wasn't raining,
this would be the first morning

without Grandma.

Sleeve

A boy's playing with the sleeve of a jacket. He winds
it around his neck, presses it to his face,
and lays it on his arm. He's peeping inside it

as if it's a telescope. He's trying to inflate it. The boy
is playing with the sleeve of his one-armed
father's jacket. They look like me and my God.

Father's Leaving

Rain rings against the panes,
autumnal rain rings.

A bee circles a clover.
And my father's

leaving. He was as strong as bread,
but has changed into a crumb.

I place him on my lips
and I can taste the loaf. Father's

leaving. I thought he'd
turn around again,

to see if I were watching.
But he walked firmly

on his fragile legs,
with the fluttering flag

of his heart. I waited for him to
look back, but perhaps he was afraid

I'd see him crying.
Or maybe it was just that

something was drawing him harder.

Hair

I can see dad standing in the doorway,
growing a little impatient as
he waits for mom, who's
fixing her hair before the mirror,
making sure every strand
is in its proper place.

Today at his graveside
I caught sight of mom
unconsciously fixing her hair
in the mirror of black granite.

Deep in my heart I smiled
at my father, and at once I sensed
what underlies the triumph
of beauty over decay.

Winter, Night

Shattered keyboard of the city
beneath credulous, illiterate snow.
Removing a crumb of chocolate from in between
the keys, I leave a trace: "loook." Crumbs of life
fall in accidental places and change into
incomprehensible words. Don't try to understand them,
you can't know what is from the other side.
The neighbors' child has been cooing all morning. The sky
looks like an e-book screen today,
on which all the crumbs
might join to form a great book.

Renovating the Facade

Plaster falls from the walls of the Capuchin convent,
the chisels work steadily, preventing sleep. In my homeland
on the Vistula they're enthroning Jesus Christ as king,
while in a small Swiss town I'm listening to the flowers
blooming, banknotes rustling, to birds vocalizing
against global warming, and the plaster falling
from seventeenth-century convent walls. Three
aged reverend sisters recognize me by now,
they're like carrier pigeons from a decimated flock
on their final flight, they have trouble with their hearing,
so they're puzzled when I explain I can't sleep
because of the chisels steadily chipping plaster off the seventeenth-
century walls of Maria Opferung convent, thus exposing
some decaying wooden crossbeams. Meanwhile above
my homeland a rainbow rises and a joyful crowd carries
on a staff a vagina set inside the Host, from pedestals fall
statues of priests who tried to force their way into
heaven through the needle's eye of a child's anus or vulva.
Little birds are singing, honey bees are poking in the flowers
at the Capuchin convent in Zug, where three aged
reverend sisters wait patiently for their summons
to eternity. Down the promenade by a lake
that looks like Gennesaret mothers-to-be are
out for a stroll, with swollen bellies. An hour from here
possessors of life wearied by life are dying from
injections of poison. The renovation work has
lasted for three months now, and I can't sleep, though the sisters
claim the chisels only work steadily by day,
chipping plaster off the convent walls. The bells of empty
churches ring on every quarter, the bells on cows' and
sheep's necks ring almost without cease. Otherwise there's
silence, a funeral cortege of clouds, the stifling odor
of overblown wisteria and plaster from the ancient walls of

the Capuchin convent, which within the year ahead
will look like new again, if we can believe the builders
and the three reverend sisters with calcified, fragile bodies.

Perfect Day

The day was full of discipline and order.

A punctual sun, birds at even intervals
on the high-tension wires.

Without a murmur the wind scattered flocks of clouds.

You took me to the rabbit cages. One of them
pricked up its ears when I said: "Why not
let them all go?" It was really a

rhetorical question. But I'm still haunted by
that glint in its eye, the quiver of its ear.

"What about letting them go?" the SS officer might have
rhetorically asked as he walked past
a barrack full of ears.

★ ★ ★

Before the sun went down, the sea on a tide
of shallow feelings cast up
at my feet:

a branch,
a dead bird,
a piece of polished glass.

It nudged me with its nose and hissed: Well then,
do something with that.

Tension and Resistance

Asked at a poetry festival whether
a poem can be a form of
resistance, I retorted: It can,

just as its banks are a form of
resistance for a river, a bird is
a form of resistance for the wind,

an electrical wire
a form of resistance for
a stream of electrons.

A stream of language runs into
resistance in poetry
and for a moment turns

into a poem, which quivers, wails,
sings, plays, and sometimes
is silent. I guess

that was my answer
to the question. It's also possible
that I sat without a word,

thinking about a cable
stretched above the meadows
that sings in the freezing

wind, although there flows
through it the news of someone's
death, amorous babbling,

all the world's jabber.

Two Clocks

On the stone gateway to Charles Bridge a lion
transformed by rains and wind
into a lump of dough.

On the walls clear sharp slashes like a rain
of freeze-frame
sparks.

The marks of soldiers who five centuries ago
sharpened their halberds on the wall for lack
of a better occupation.

One of those sparks jumps across from then
to now under the nose of the lion,
who was going to roar out to us

the danger of transience.

A Poem Made of Gum

The point is to have a
shapeless piece of gum,
which we can carry
in our pocket and gnaw on,
and that will remind us
of the most important thing.

The point is to have a
shapeless piece of gum,
which we can carry
in our pocket and gnaw on,
and that will remind us
of the most important thing.

The point is to have a
shapeless piece of gum,
which we can carry
in our pocket and gnaw on,
and that will remind us
that in the other pocket

we're already carrying a shapeless
piece of gum that we can
carry in our pocket and gnaw on,
and that reminded us
of the most important thing.

Guide

Walking to the night store for another bottle
I spotted a guide to Polish literature
for high-school students, it was more worn-out
than I am, lying face down, it looked

like a fallen angel, Icarus, or someone who's
hugging the sidewalk, whatever. It crossed my mind
that if I picked it up and spotted my own name
in the index, I'd turn back, I swear to God, I'd turn back

home (and you must know it has been in the
guides before). I picked it up and found nothing.

Though I pass that book each night.

The Literary Journals' Farewell

For Adam Zagajewski

I dreamed I had a craving for a literary
journal, the way one craves a freshly
baked loaf, I strayed around the local kiosks,
but all they had was daily news and crosswords,
until at last in a booth on the fringes
of the world a vendor with a voice as bittersweet
as a song by Schubert, with the face of Adam
Zagajewski, said to me: "Tadeusz, don't
compare me with Schubert," and handed me
a copy of a literary journal, which
stands still unopened on my shelf today,
crammed between the books like a slice of bread.

Inspiration

I spent a month with poets of every race,
we talked of love, of writing, diseases, and of wars,
we ate together, wandered around the town,
and phoned our loved ones at much the same times.

Once I got back home I was convinced
poets surrounded me on every side, but
when I asked an incidental passer-by:
"What are you writing now?" I heard: "Beat it,

screwball." And then it dawned on me that this
person was mad because he was waiting for
inspiration.

Squirrel

There are three stages in the life of a poet. First
he plays the role of a poet, "I am a poet," he says
to the mirror before each public reading,
admiring his own nuts.

The second stage is being a poet for real. He loses
his stage fright, he starts to think of writing
as a job, his hollow tree-trunk turns into an office,
he builds contacts, sees to business,
cites his own experience and willingly
gives talks of the "my ars poetica" kind.
One must admit that in this stage he's the wisest
in his entire career, but also the dullest.

The third stage relies––again––on playing
the role of a poet, but not from the position of one
who's not quite up to it, but one who
can leave aside so-called
literary life. He gains greater
joy from things not said than from confidences,
he's bored by tirades, he practices small talk.

Only now does he feel truly free.
He walks across the park and, smiling to himself,
watches a poem, as just like a squirrel
it vanishes behind the bough of a tree.

There is a War On

At noon in Poland nothing but private soldiers,
but morale is rising, that night the privates
are promoted to commanders, at around 10:00 p.m.
we have in the country some ten million
commanders, who with the use of a remote control
redeploy the troops, whole divisions, around
midnight every third Polish man (and
maybe woman, if the man allows
her to fight), is a drone operator by now
and simultaneously puts up resistance on the streets
with the help of some six-packs of Tyskie beer
or a western weapon, a Heineken, which strikes
more precisely, but regrettably more slowly.
The Polish military wake in the morning with
significant losses in supplies and
lowered morale. They've only enough forces
for a Polish-Polish war. But they bravely head off
for ammunition to the nearby convenience store,
and on the way they wage war. They're having a mental fight.

Being Sure

I've been to the town of Boneville, but I don't know what for.
It flashed past on the internet, and at once I felt sure
I'd spent at least a day and a night there. I'm sure I
read my poems, then I did some drinking, and then I fell in love
with a Boneville girl, made love to a Boneville girl or to myself.
  I'm sure
I went to church, and then I had another dream
that I'd earned hundreds of dollars in Boneville for my
poems. I'd talked about Boneville to my friends
and family. No one was surprised. I have been
—as sure as I'm alive—to Boneville,
though I don't know when and what for.

Comet

"Just lately we were together at the graves"
or: "He said we'd see each other in a week
at the barbecue—such comments about my death intrude
on me every day (their frequency calls for

professional help), but sometime one of them is sure
to materialize on someone's tongue, just as
I too materialized one fine day,
exactly forty-two years ago like a comet in the sky,

from which now and then there break off
great and small phrases.

A Song about Traction

First you load requests into your devotions
like cargo into a railcar, the overburdened rolling stock
heaves toward the port of New Heaven so sluggishly
that half the goods pass their expiry date. Later

you start to realize that the content of the cars
is not weighty, so you send them off empty,
entire rosaries roll towards New Heaven,
and the mere sound of them reassures you. Until at last

the railcars cease to interest you, you're keeping an eye on
the timetable, that's enough to avoid coming off the rails.
And then you suddenly notice you've lost the attraction
of prayer, after all, you've long since been living with the family

in New Heaven. Go then onto the loading ramp and get back down
to grueling physical labor.

Creative Reading

I remember the day when I gave you a volume
by Charles Bukowski with some poems marked.
When you read them, you got scared that
in this tortuous way I was trying to drop you. Later

we were married, to divorce after a number of years,
as fine and fruitless as creative writing courses.
Today those poems fell into my hands again, I'm reading
them at random, cautiously, to avoid doing you harm.

Bungee Cord

Under the quilt of sleep lies the poet, as precise
as tautology in committing the errors
of a lifetime, for he never makes moral or grammatical
mistakes, since mastering the art of constructing
metaphors, behind which he can hide from
himself, so there he lies, devising another poem,
in which the level of sincerity surpasses the content
of truth in reality, as a way of buying himself
out of the verdicts of conscience again, though now too
he knows, jumping on the bungee cord of language into the chasm
in himself, that he's ever closer to the sheet of water,
in which for a moment he can make out his own
reflection, or even smash it with his head. But
the water level is dropping, and the rope is fraying.

Why Poetry is Essential to You for Life

Because it floats around the station like a pretty junkie whom
you'd be happy to screw, if not for your position.

Or it laughs in your face like a child that you'd
pamper if it were yours. Or it causes trouble

like a decrepit mother who can't remember a thing,
who craps herself, whom you'd bury alive in the woods

if not for your love for her and your position.
Or it spoils your mood like a fortune-teller who

accurately predicts your wasted past. Poetry
is necessary to you so sometimes you can

get out of yourself, see, and never return.

The Scent of Man

They sat in my compartment,
two couples of an indefinable
age. They smelled of yesterday's
and tomorrow's alcohol, cheap tobacco
and heroic helplessness. The woman opposite
me must have had lovely features, before
they were plowed up by a long gang bang with ethanol
and acetaldehyde. Each individually
did not yet stink, only as a foursome
did they release the odor of one bona fide
bum. The question flashed through my mind,
what does humankind smell like, and would its
clean part be able, like a gigantic
bar of toilet soap, to smother the nasty
stench of the rest, to shut their decay
in an airtight coffin of perfume. And where
in the midst of all this does my own smell float.

Meaning

I am the level-crossing attendant at a forgotten station,
I let through one train a week, my work
has meaning.

My television shows a snowstorm on all two
channels, but even so I know more about this world
than I'd like.

At Christmas I fetch an artificial tree from the closet,
with stuck-on baubles, it's a pity to waste
time on the same thing each year.

The rain plays on my roof, the wind on my lightning rod.

I see my wife rarely, she can't understand
trains, especially the ones that run once
a week. I'm told my daughter is building a career
in the capital, but I think she's just sleeping around.

On occasions when I'm pensive the distant prairie trail
blends into one with the top of the dado rail.

Actually I don't get bored, when a person's alone
for long enough, boredom disappears. In the past
I did it all on my own, staring at the moon,
but then I stopped, because what's the pleasure

if you don't have to hide. I love the sound of shuddering
rails, I always hear it whenever something
important is to happen in my life. Today

on television they talked about poetry.
I don't know what a poet can do if he doesn't write.
I'd like someone to write a poem about me one day.

Oh, I think it's on its way.

Resin

The mother with a baby in her arms,
waiting in line for bread,

and God's own musician
rapping out his

disappointed loves
on a chair by the subway entrance.

The student who spends his time
at an eternal party, and the

watchmaker who makes sure
the clock never runs behind

by more than three seconds
a day. They are all

immersed in meaning
like flies in the still liquid

resin of life. Their motions
will determine

who shall remain in amber,
and who shall not.

What Does String Theory Entail

It entails a poet pulling on one of them,
extracting a seductive sound,

and when he lets it go, it strikes against others,
and worlds interpenetrate, miracles occur,

of which the philosophers never dreamed, "that's
impossible"—people say,

on seeing their parents dying, and their children
starting to walk. Then everything returns

to its place; the scientists think up
far-fetched creations, poets write with toil.

Communion

In a cluster of youthful heads,
resembling a clump of honey
mushrooms, I find my own,
I'm looking defiantly into the lens,
like into a hyper-spatial tunnel.

A black-and-white photo
of my First Holy Communion—
I found it at the bottom of a drawer,
while sorting things out for my divorce.

The boy in front of me has gone,
he smashed against the rocks
while rafting on a river of
vodka. The one with his mouth open,
a missionary in the Argentine,
was killed in an accident, trying
to swerve past a wild swine
in the road or in himself.

My life too has ended
many times over. Now I'm
doing all I can to return
to my pew. To forget.
But as I look into the eyes
of that same boy, I can see
he wants to jump out of himself.

To anywhere, if only into me.

About the Author

TADEUSZ DĄBROWSKI (b. 1979) Poet, essayist, critic. Editor-in-chief of the literary bimonthly *Topos*. He has been published in *The New Yorker*, *Paris Review*, *Boston Review*, *Threepenny Review*, *Ploughshares*, *Agni*, *American Poetry Review*, *Poetry Daily*, *Guernica*, among others. Recipient of stipends awarded by Yaddo (2015), the Omi International Arts Center (NY, 2013), and the Vermont Studio Center (2011). Winner of numerous awards, among others, the Kościelski Prize (2009), the Hubert Burda Prize (2008) and, from Tadeusz Różewicz, the Prize of the Foundation for Polish Culture (2006). He has been nominated for the NIKE Award (2010). His work has been translated into 30 languages. Author of ten volumes of poetry in his native Polish, from which the most recent are *Scrabble* (2020) and *To jest fajka* (2022) [This is a pipe], and a dozen in translation. He has also published a novel, *Bezbronna kreska* (2016) [Defenseless line], set in New York City, and a collection of essays on poetry, entitled *In Metaphor* (2024). Two of his collections, *Black Square* and *POSTS*, have been published in English by Zephyr Press. He lives in Gdańsk on the Baltic coast of Poland.

About the Translator

 ANTONIA LLOYD-JONES has translated works by many of Poland's leading contemporary novelists and reportage authors, as well as classics, biographies, essays, crime fiction, poetry and children's books. Her notable translations include *Drive Your Plow Over the Bones of the Dead* by 2018 Nobel Prize laureate Olga Tokarczuk. Her most recent work includes *My Name is Stramer*, a novel by Mikołaj Łoziński, and as compiler and co-translator, *The Penguin Book of Polish Short Stories*.

Acknowledgments

These poems first appeared in the following journals:

Boston Review, June 12, 2023: "Communion," "What Does
        String Theory Entail"

Cyphers, issue 91: "Grammar," "This is the End"

Image, issue 91: "Jam Jars"
      issue 126: "Boots," "A Song about Traction"

The New Yorker, July 22, 2019: "Sentence"
            October 26, 2020: "Letter"
            January 3 & 10, 2022: "Bouquet"
            April 17, 2023: "Break"

The Paris Review, issue 230, 2019: "Hall of Mirrors,"
      "Secret Reading Matter"
      issue 238, 2021: "Hilltop"

The Threepenny Review, issue 175, 2023: "Snake"
            issue 182, 2025: "Bungee Cord"

Books by

ARROWSMITH

PRESS

Girls by Oksana Zabuzhko

Bula Matari/Smasher of Rocks by Tom Sleigh

This Carrying Life by Maureen McLane

Cries of Animals Dying by Lawrence Ferlinghetti

Animals in Wartime by Matiop Wal

Divided Mind by George Scialabba

The Jinn by Amira El-Zein

Bergstein
edited by Askold Melnyczuk

Arrow Breaking Apart by Jason Shinder

Beyond Alchemy by Daniel Berrigan

Conscience, Consequence: Reflections on Father Daniel Berrigan
edited by Askold Melnyczuk

Ric's Progress by Donald Hall

Return To The Sea by Etnairis Rivera

The Kingdom of His Will by Catherine Parnell

Eight Notes from the Blue Angel by Marjana Savka

Fifty-Two by Melissa Green

Music In—And On—The Air by Lloyd Schwartz

Magpiety by Melissa Green

Reality Hunger by William Pierce

Soundings: On The Poetry of Melissa Green
edited by Sumita Chakraborty

The Corny Toys by Thomas Sayers Ellis

Black Ops by Martin Edmunds

Museum of Silence by Romeo Oriogun

City of Water by Mitch Manning

Passeggiate by Judith Baumel

Persephone Blues by Oksana Lutsyshyna

The Uncollected Delmore Schwartz
edited by Ben Mazer

The Light Outside by George Kovach

The Blood of San Gennaro by Scott Harney
edited by Megan Marshall

No Sign by Peter Balakian

Firebird by Kythe Heller

The Selected Poems of Oksana Zabuzhko
edited by Askold Melnyczuk

The Age of Waiting by Douglas J. Penick

Manimal Woe by Fanny Howe

Crank Shaped Notes by Thomas Sayers Ellis

The Land of Mild Light by Rafael Cadenas
edited by Nidia Hernández

The Silence of Your Name: The Afterlife of a Suicide by Alexandra Marshall

Flame in a Stable by Martin Edmunds

Mrs. Schmetterling by Robin Davidson

This Costly Season by John Okrent

Thorny by Judith Baumel

The Invisible Borders of Time: Five Female Latin American Poets
edited by Nidia Hernández

Some of You Will Know by David Rivard

The Forbidden Door: The Selected Poetry of Lasse Söderberg
tr. by Lars Gustaf Andersson & Carolyn Forché

Unrevolutionary Times by Houman Harouni

Between Fury & Peace: The Many Arts of Derek Walcott
edited by Askold Melnyczuk

The Burning World by Sherod Santos

New and Selected Poems by Glyn Maxwell

A Precise Chaos by Jo-Ann Mort

Where Do You Live? by Jennifer Jean

Coming Ashore by Thomas O'Grady

Crimean Fig / Qırım İnciri
edited by Anastasia Levkova, Askold Melnyczuk,
& Nataliya Shpylova-Saeed

ARROWSMITH is named after the late William Arrowsmith, a renowned classics scholar, literary and film critic. General editor of thirty-three volumes of *The Greek Tragedy in New Translations*, he was also a brilliant translator of Eugenio Montale, Cesare Pavese, and others. Arrowsmith, who taught for years in Boston University's University Professors Program, championed not only the classics and the finest in contemporary literature, he was also passionate about the importance of recognizing the translator's role in bringing the original work to life in a new language.

Like the arrowsmith who turns his arrows straight and true,
a wise person makes his character straight and true.   —Buddha